Anonymous

Almanac and Annual Diary and Memoranda for 1864

Anonymous

Almanac and Annual Diary and Memoranda for 1864

ISBN/EAN: 9783337021344

Printed in Europe, USA, Canada, Australia, Japan

Cover: Foto ©ninafisch / pixelio.de

More available books at **www.hansebooks.com**

ALMANAC

AND

ANNUAL DIARY

SIC SEMPER TYRANNIS.

AND

MEMORANDA

FOR 1864.

Lynchburg, Va:
JOHNSON & SCHAFFTER,
PUBLISHERS.

Eclipses for the year 1864.

First.—Of the Sun, May the 5th, at 7h. 4m. afternoon. invisible.

Second.—Of the Sun, October 30th, at 10h 11m. in the morning, invisible.

Common Notes for the year 1864.

Chronological Cycles.	*Movable Feasts.*
Dominical Letters......C & B	Ash Wednesday........Feb. 10
Golden Number................3	Easter Sunday.......March 27
Epact...............................2	Ascension Day........March 5
Solar Cycle 25	Whitsunday..............May 15
Roman Indiction.............7	Trinity Sunday........May 22
Julian Period................6577	Advent Sunday...... Nov'r 27

Morning and Evening Stars.

The Planet Venus will be morning star till July 18th; then evening star to the end of the year

The Planet Jupiter will be morning star till May 13th; then evening star till Nov. 30th; then morning star again.

The Planet Saturn will be morning star till April 4th; than evening star till October 14th; then morning star to the end of the year.

True Time.

Two kinds of time are used in Almanacs ; *clock* or *mean time* in some, and *apparent* or *sun-time* in others. *Clock*-time is always *right*, while *Sun*-time varies every day. People generally suppose it is twelve o'clock when the sun is due south, or at a properly made noon-mark. But this is a mistake. The sun is seldom on the meridian at 12 o'clock ; indeed this is the case only on four days of the year: namely. April 15, June 15, Sept. 1 and Dec. 24. In this Almanac, the time used is *clock*-time. The time when the sun is on the meridian or at the noon-mark is also given to the nearest second in the "CONCISE EQUATION TABLE," on page third of this Almanac. This affords a ready means of obtaining correct time and for setting a clock by using a noon-mark, adding or subtracting as the sun is slow or fast.

Old fashioned Almanacs, which use *apparent* time, give the rising and setting of the sun's *centre* and make no allowance for the effect of refraction of the sun's rays by the atmosphere. The more modern and improved Almanacs, which use clock-time, give the rising and setting of the sun's upper limb, and duly allow for refraction. See table page third.

Never speak ill of any one, on any pretence whatever.

Concise Equation Table,

Showing to the nearest minute how much a clock should be faster or slower than a sun-dial or noon-mark.

Add to Dial Time.			Subtract from Dial Time.		
Date.		Min.	Date.		Min
December	26	1	April	18	1
Do.	28	2	"	22	2
Do.	30	3	"	28	3
January	1	4	May	5	4
Do.	5	5	"	24	3
Do.	6	6	June	2	2
Do.	7	7	"	8	1
Do.	9	8	September	3	1
Do.	12	9	"	6	2
Do.	15	10	"	9	3
Do.	18	11	"	12	4
Do.	21	12	"	14	5
Do.	25	13	"	17	6
Do.	30	14	"	20	7
February	10	15	"	23	8
Do.	13	14	"	26	9
Do.	24	13	"	29	10
March	2	12	October	2	11
Do.	6	11	"	5	12
Do.	10	10	"	9	13
Do.	14	9	"	13	14
Do.	17	8	"	17	15
Do.	21	7	"	23	16
Do.	24	6	November	14	15
Do.	27	5	"	19	14
Do.	31	4	"	23	13
April	4	3	"	26	12
Do.	7	2	"	29	11
Do.	11	1	December	2	10
June	17	1	"	5	9
Do.	22	2	"	7	8
Do.	27	3	"	9	7
July	2	4	"	11	6
Do.	7	5	"	13	5
Do.	14	6	"	16	4
August	7	5	"	18	3
Do.	14	4	"	20	2
Do.	19	3	"	22	1
Do.	23	2			
Do.	27	1			

We have introduced this table in its most simple dress. It should thus be engraven upon every well-constructed family Sun-Dial.

Herschel's Weather Table,

For foretelling the Weather, throughout all the lunation of each year, forever.

This Table and the accompanying remarks are the result of many years' actual observation, the whole being constructed on a due consideration of the attraction of the sun and moon, in their several positions respecting the earth, and will, by simple inspection, show the observer what kind of weather will most probably follow the entrance of the moon into any of its quarters, and that so near the truth as to be seldom or never found to fail.

If the new moon, 1t qr., full moon or last qr. happens	In Summer	In winter.
Bet. midnight & 2.	Fair	Frost unless w. s.-w.
2 and 4 morning....	Cold—showers..	Snow and stormy.
4 and 6 "	Rain	Rain.
6 and 8 "	Wind and rain..	Stormy. [snow if e
8 and 10 "	Changeable......	Cold rain if wind w..
10 and 12 "	Freq't showers	Cold and high wind.
12 and 2 afternoon	Very rainy	Snow or rain.
2 and 4...............	Changeable..... ..	Fair and mild.
4 and 6...............	Fair	Fair. [n. or n. e.
6 and 8...............	Fair if wind n.w	Fair and frosty if w'd
8 and 10...............	Rainy if s.-s.w..	Rain or snow if s. or
10 and midnight....	Fair	Fair and frosty. [s. w.

OBSERVATIONS.—1. The nearer the time of the moon's change, first quarter, full and last quarter are to *midnight* the fairer will be the weather during the next 7 days.

2. The space for this calculation occupies from ten at night till two next morning.

3. The nearer to *midday* or *noon*, the phases of the moon happens, the more foul or wet weather may be expected during the next seven days.

4. The space for this calculation occupies from ten in the forenoon to two in the afternoon. These observations refer principally to the summer, though they effect spring and autumn nearly in the same ratio.

5. The moon's change, first quarter, full and last quarter, happening during six of the afternoon hours, *i. e.* from four to ten, may be followed by fair weather; but this is mostly dependent on the *wind*, as is noted in the table.

6. Though the weather, from a variety of irregular causes, is more uncertain in the latter part of autumn, the whole of winter, and the beginning of spring, yet in the main the above observations will apply to those periods also.

7. To prognosticate correctly, especially in those cases where the *wind* is concerned, the observer should be within sight of a good *vane*, where the four cardinal points of the heavens are correctly placed.

Moon's Phases.

	d.	h.	m.	
Last Quarter	1	10	0	after.
New Moon	9	2	32	morn.
First Quarter	15	11	28	after.
Full Moon	23	4	36	after.
Last Quarter	31	1	43	after.

d. m.	d. w.	REMARKABLE DAYS.	Sun Rises.	Sun Sets.	Moon Rises.
			H. M.	H. M.	H. M.
1	fr	Sun in perigee	7 16	4 44	morn
2	sat	Conj. moon with Sat	16 ..	4 40	14
3	E	Moon 23 days old	15 ..	45 1	12
4	mo	Venus rises 3 40 morn	15 ..	45 2	12
5	tue	British dis. Rich'd 1781	15 ..	45 3	14
6	we	Epiphany	14 ..	46 4	17
7	thu	Luna runs low	14 ..	46 5	18
8	fri	Battle N. O. 1815	13 ..	47 6	14
9	sat	Florida & Mississippi ⎫	12 ..	48	sets
10	E	seceded, 1861 ⎭	12 ..	48 6	55
11	mo	Alabama seceded, '61	11 ..	49 8	8
12	tue	Moon lat. 5 deg. N	11 ..	49 9	22
13	we	Moon on the equator	10 ..	50 10	28
14	thu	Moon five days old	9 ..	51 11	32
15	fri	Sirius south 10 51	9 ..	51	morn
16	sat	Battle Ironton, '62	8 ..	52 0	36
17	E	Franklin born, 1706	7 ..	53 1	36
18	mo	John Tyler died '62	6 ..	54 2	35
19	tue	Georgia seceded '61	6 ..	54 3	30
20	we	Sun enters aquarius	5 ..	55 4	24
21	thu	Moon twelve days old	4 ..	56 5	12
22	fri	Day's increase 30 min	3 ..	57 5	47
23	sat	Wm. Pitt died 1806	3 ..	57	rises
24	E	Septuagesima	2 ..	58 6	12
25	mo	Moon's lat. 5° 9' south	1 ..	59 7	8
26	tue	Day ten hours long	0 5	0 8	3
27	we	Saturn rises 10 52	6 59 ..	1 8	58
28	thu	Moon nineteen days old	58 ..	2 9	55
29	fri	Conj. Moon with saturn	57 ..	3 10	54
30	sat	Charles I beheaded 1648	56 ..	4 11	54
31	E	Sexagesima	55 ..	5	morn

☞ Mississippi Search Warrant is the polite name for a fine tooth comb in the army.

6   February, 1864.

Moon's Phases.

	d.	h.	m.	
New Moon	7	0	56	after.
First Quarter	14	1	33	after.
Full Moon	22	11	54	morn.

d. m.	d. w	REMARKABLE DAYS.	Sun Rises.		Sun Sets.		Moon Rises.	
			H.	M.	H.	M	H.	M.
1	mo	Conj. moon with Jup....	6	54	5	0 0	0	54
2	tue	Moon 24 days old..........	..	53	..	7 1	55	
3	we	Luna runs low	..	52	..	8 2	55	
4	thu	Provisional Congress)	..	51	..	9 3	55	
5	fri	C. S? met 1861....... }	..	50	..	10 4	48	
6	sat	Venus rises 4 29 morn..	..	49	..	11 5	37	
7	E	Quinquagesima	..	48	..	12 6	20	
8	mo	Fall of Roanoke Isl. '62	..	47	..	13	sets	
9	tue	Federals at Florence	..	46	..	14 8	4	
10	we	Ash Wednesday	..	45	..	15 9	9	
11	thu	Saturn rises 9 52............	..	44	..	16 10	16	
12	fri	Days increase 1 h. 10 m..	..	43	..	17 11	19	
13	sat	Battle Fort Donelson '62	..	42	..	18	morn	
14	E	St. Valentine's Day......	..	41	..	19 0	18	
15	mo	Sirius south 8 42............	..	40	..	20 1	15	
16	tue	Sur. Fort Donelson, '62.	..	39	..	21 2	10	
17	we	Luna runs high.............	..	37	..	23 3	2	
18	thu	Moon ten days old.........	..	36	..	24 3	48	
19	fri	Battle Mill Spring, '62..	..	35	..	25 4	30	
20	sat	Moon in Apogee...........	..	34	..	26 5	8	
21	E	Moon's lat. 5 90 south..	..	32	..	28 5	43	
22	mo	Jeff. Davis inaug. '62....	..	31	..	29	rises	
23	tue	Battle Buena Vista, '49.	..	30	..	30 6	49	
24	we	Day 11 h. 2 m. long......	..	29	..	31 7	46	
25	thu	Day's increase 1 40......	..	28	..	32 8	44	
26	fri	Conj. moon with Saturn	..	27	..	33 9	44	
27	sat	Moon 19 days old..........	..	26	..	34 10	44	
28	E	Third Sunday in Lent....	..	25	..	35 11	45	
29	mo	Saturn rises 11 47..........	..	24	..	.36	morn	

☞ A preacher down South said. "O Lord! we pray thee to curtail the devil's power in this place;" when an old negro, always ready with a response, exclaimed, "Dat right. Lord, cut he tail smack smoove off!"

☞ A teetotaller said he could not marry a wife because his principles would not allow him to sup-*porter*.

Moon's Phases.

	d.	h.	m.	
Last Quarter	1	2	51	morn.
New Moon	7	10	58	after.
First Quarter	15	4	54	morn.
Full Moon	23	5	28	morn.
Last Quarter	30	1	29	after.

d. m.	d. w.	Remarkable Days.	Sun Rises.		Sun Sets.		Moon Rises.	
			H.	M.	H.	M.	H.	M.
1	tue	Czar Nicholas died 1855	6	28	5	37	0	43
2	we	John Wesley died 1791		22		38	1	45
3	thu	Moon 24 days old		21		39	2	46
4	fri	First U. S. Cong. met		20		44	3	43
5	sat	1781		19		41	4	31
6	L	Moon's lat. 5 7 north		17		43	5	17
7	mo	Battle Elkhorn 1862		16		44	5	54
8	tue	Naval engagement in		15		45	sets	
9	we	Hampton Roads '62		14		46	8	5
10	thu	Days increase 2 12		12		48	9	10
11	fri	Surnames first used 1072		11		49	10	11
12	sat	Moon 4 days old		10		50	11	9
13	L	Fifth Sunday in Lent		9		51	morn	
14	mo	Luna runs high,		8		52	0	3
15	tue	And. Jackson born 1767		7		53	0	57
16	we	Procyon sou. 7 40		6		54	1	47
17	thu	St. Patrick's Day		5		55	2	31
18	fri	Moon 10 days old		3		57	3	11
19	sat	Moon in Apogee		2		58	3	50
20	L	Palm Sunday,		0	6	0	4	24
21	mo	Days and nights equal 5	5	59		1	4	57
22	tue	Moon on the equator		58		2	5	27
23	we	Texas admitted 1861		57		3	rises	
24	thu	Battle Kernstown 1862		55		5	7	36
25	fri	Good Friday		54		6	8	37
26	sat	Lady's Day		53		7	9	38
27	L	Easter Sunday		52		8	10	39
28	mo	Bruce crowned 1306		51		9	11	39
29	tue	Moon lowest		50		10	morn	
30	we	Moon 22 days old		49		11	0	37
31	thu	Days increase 3 34		48		12	1	29

☞ Never fish for praise; it is not worth the bait.

Moon's Phases.

	d.	h.	m.
New Moon	6	8	51 morn.
First Quarter	13	9	4 after.
Full Moon	21	7	53 after.
Last Quarter	28	10	1 after.

d. m.	d. w.	REMARKABLE DAYS.	Sun Rises.		Sun Sets.		Moon Rises.	
			H.	M.	H.	M.	H.	M.
1	fri	All Fool's Day	5	46	6	14	2	21
2	sat	Moon in Perigree	..	45	..	15	3	6
3	E	Low Sunday	..	44	..	16	3	45
4	mo	Gen. Harrison died '41.	..	43	..	17	4	20
5	tue	Saturn south 11 58	..	41	..	19	4	54
6	we	Battle Shiloh, '62	..	40	..	20		sets
7	thu	Venus rises 4 28	..	39	..	21	8	6
8	fri	Island No. 10 sur. '62	..	38	..	22	9	9
9	sat	Lord Bacon died 1626	..	36	..	24	10	7
10	E	Luna runs high,	..	35	..	25	11	3
11	mo	Moon five days old	..	34	..	26	11	54
12	tue	Bom. Fort Sumter '61	..	33	..	27		morn
13	we	Day 12 56 long	..	32	..	28	0	39
14	thu	Embargo repealed '14	..	31	..	29	1	21
15	fri	Moon's lat. 5 7 south	..	30	..	30	1	59
16	sat	Moon in Apogee	..	29	..	31	2	28
17	E	3d Sunday after Easter	..	28	..	32	3	0
18	mo	Virginia admitted '61	..	26	..	34	3	29
19	tue	Balt. massacre, '61	..	25	..	35	3	58
20	we	Sun enters Venus	..	24	..	36	4	28
21	thu	Moon fifteen days old	..	23	..	37		rises
22	fri	Battle Camden 1781	..	22	..	38	7	38
23	sat	S. Car. ratified consti-	..	21	..	39	8	38
24	E	tution C. S. '61	..	20	..	40	9	38
25	mo	Va. rat. constitution '61	..	19	..	41	10	38
26	tue	Day's increase 4 hours	..	18	..	42	11	31
27	we	Fed. troops at N. O. '62	..	17	..	43		morn
28	thu	Wolfe killed, 1759,	..	16	..	44	0	20
29	fri	Moon in perigree	..	15	..	45	1	8
30	sat	Washington inaug 1789	..	14	..	46	1	48

☞ Among the Romans the gift of a ring was a badge of liberation from slavery. Married people can best explain whether it is so amongst the moderns.

Moon's Phases.

	d.	h.	m.	
New Moon	5	7	4	after.
First Quarter	13	1	17	after.
Full Moon	21	8	2	morn.
Last Quarter	28	5	25	morn.

d. m.	d. w.	REMARKABLE DAYS.	Sun Rises.	Sun Sets.	Moon Rises.
			H. M	H. M.	H. M.
1	E	Rogation Sunday......... 5	13 6	47 2	25
2	mo	Bat. Chancellorsville ⎱ ..	12 ..	48 2	59
3	tue	on the 2d and 3d, '63 ⎰ ..	11 ..	49 3	35
4	we	Saturn south 10 6......... ..	10 ..	50 4	11
5	thu	Bonaparte died '21......... ..	9 ..	51 4	51
6	fri	Battle Jamestown '62	8 ..	52	sets
7	sat	Gen. Worth died '49...... ..	7 ..	53.8	59
8	E	Battle McDowell '62...... ..	6 ..	54 9	50
9	mo	Blockade Va. begun '61.....	5 ..	55 10	38
10	tue	General T. J. Jackson ⎱ ..	4 ..	56 11	20
11	we	died '63,............... ⎰ ..	3 ..	57	morn
12	thu	Day's increase 4 32,........ ..	2 ..	58 0	0
13	fri	Moon in Apogee........... ..	1 ..	59 0	35
14	sat	Day fourteen hours long ..	0 7	0 1	6
15	E	Whit Sunday 4	59 ..	1 1	36
16	mo	Moon ten days old......... ..	58 ..	2 2	5
17	tue	Revolu in Venice, 1767.... ..	57 ..	3 2	32
18	we	Matamoras taken, '46	57 ..	3 3	2
19	thu	Venus rises 4 6 morn..... ..	56 ..	4 3	33
20	fri	Sun enters Gemini......... ..	55 ..	5 4	12
21	sat	Moon fifteen days old..... ..	55 ..	5	rises
22	E	Trinity Sunday	54 ..	6 8	22
23	mo	Battle Front Royal, '62. ..	53 ..	7 9	19
24	tue	Victoria born, '19......... ..	53 ..	7 10	10
25	we	Moon nineteen days old ..	52 ..	8 10	57
26	thu	Moon's lat. 5 6 north...... ..	51 ..	9 11	40
27	fri	Moon in Perigee........... ..	51 ..	9,	morn
28	sat	N. Carolina admitted '61 ..	50 ..	10 0	18
29	E	Pres. Davis arrived in ⎱ ..	49 ..	11 0	53
30	mo	Richmond, '61...... ⎰ ..	49 ..	11 1	32
31	tue	Battle Seven Pines, '62.... ..	48 ..	12 2	8

Had Adam been modern, there would have been a hired girl in Paradise to look out for little Abel and 'raise Cain.'

June, 1864.

Moon's Phases.

	d.	h.	m.	
New Moon	4	6	18	morn.
First Quarter	12	5	28	morn.
Full Moon	19	5	33	after.
Last Quarter	26	0	40	after.

d. m	d. w	REMARKABLE DAYS.	Sun Rises.		Sun Sets.		Moon Rises.	
			H.	M.	H.	M.	H.	M.
1	we	Battle Seven Pines, '62..	4	48	7	12	2	45
2	thu	Day's increase 5 2	..	47	..	13	3	25
3	fri	Jeff. Davis born 1808...	..	47	..	13	4	9
4	sat	Luna runs high	..	46	..	14	sets	
5	E	2d Sunday after Trinity	..	46	..	14	8	26
6	mo	Patrick Henry died 1799	..	45	..	15	9	15
7	tue	W. B Mumford hung '62	..	45	..	15	9	54
8	we	And. Jackson died '45...	..	44	..	16	10	31
9	thu	Battle Port Republic '62	..	44	..	16	11	3
10	fri	Battle Bethel '61	..	44	..	16	11	32
11	sat	Moon seven days old	..	43	..	16	morn	
12	E	3d Sunday after Trinity	..	43	..	17	0	1
13	mo	Conj Moon with Jupit'r	..	43	..	17	0	30
14	tue	Venus rises 4 5 morn	..	43	..	17	1	0
15	we	James K. Polk died '49.	..	43	..	17	1	30
16	thu	Conj. Moon with Saturn	..	42	..	18	2	1
17	fri	Battle Bunker Hill 1775	..	42	..	18	2	40
18	sat	Battle Waterloo '15	..	42	..	18	3	27
19	E	4th Sunday after Trinity	..	42	..	18	rises	
20	mo	Queen Victoria crowned	..	42	..	18	7	57
21	tue	Summer Solstice }	..	42	..	18	8	48
22	we	Longest day }	..	42	..	18	9	34
23	thu	Moon's lat. 5 7 north	..	42	..	18	10	15
24	fri	St. John Baptist	..	42	..	18	10	50
25	sat	Moon on the equator	..	42	..	18	11	24
26	E	Battle near Richmond,	..	42	..	18	morn	
27	mo	from 26th to 30th, '62	..	43	..	17	0	0
28	tue	Madison died '36	..	43	..	17	0	37
29	we	Henry Clay died 52	..	43	..	17	1	17
30	thu	Montezuma died 1520	..	43	..	17	1	58

☞ The curious man goes about to gratify his curiosity, but he will probably never travel far enough to find anything more curious than himself.

Moon's Phases.

	d.	h.	m.	
New Moon	3	6	57	after.
First Quarter	11	5	59	after.
Full Moon	19	1	20	morn.
Last Quarter	25	11	22	morn.

d. m.	d. w.	REMARKABLE DAYS.	Sun Rises.		Sun Sets.		Moon Rises.	
			H.	M.	H.	M.	H.	M.
1	fri	Battle Malvern Hill. '62	4	43	7	17	2	45
2	sat	Tennessee admitted '61....		44	..	16	3	38
3	E	Conj. Moon with Venus. ..		44	..	16	4	34
4	mo	Independence 1776.... ⎞		44	..	16	sets	
5	tue	Jefferson and Adams ⎟		45	..	15	8	23
6	we	died, 1826 ⎟		45	..	15	8	59
7	thu	Monroe died, 1831 ⎠		45	..	15	9	29
8	fri	Burke died, 1797		46	..	14	9	58
9	sat	Z. Taylor died, '50		46	..	14	10	26
10	E	Columbus born, 1447....		47	..	13	10	55
11	mo	John Q. Adams born '67		47	..	13	11	25
12	tue	Moon seven days old.....		48	..	12	11	56
13	we	Vega south 11 0		48	..	12	morn	
14	thu	Conj. Moon with Jupiter		49	..	11	0	33
15	fri	Jupiter stationary		50	..	10	1	16
16	sat	Altair south 11 58		50	..	10	2	4
17	E	8th Sunday after Trinity		51	..	9	3	0
18	mo	Battle Bull Run, '61		52	..	8	4	5
19	tue	Conj. Sun with Venus.....		52	..	8	rises	
20	we	Moon's lat. 5 9 north.....		53	..	7	8	2
21	thu	Battle Manassas, '61		54	..	6	8	39
22	fri	Sun enters Leo		55	..	5	9	16
23	sat	Moon eighteen days old....		55	..	5	9	52
24	E	9th Sunday after Trinity		56	..	4	10	28
25	mo	Bat. Lunday's Lane, '14		57	..	3	11	7
26	tue	Day 14 h. 6 m long		57	..	3	11	51
27	we	Saturn sets 10 5,		58	..	2	morn	
28	thu	Jupiter sets 11 36		59	..	1	0	38
29	fri	Luna runs high,		59	..	1	1	27
30	sat	Wm. Penn died, 1718...	5	0	..	0	2	23
31	E	10th Sunday aft. Trinity		1	6	59	3	18

Dignity does not consist in possessing honors, but in deserving them.

August, 1864.

Moon's Phases.

	d.	h.	m.	
New Moon	2	9	14	morn.
First Quarter,	10	7	44	morn.
Full Moon	17	8	34	morn.
Last Quarter,	24	4	58	morn.

d. m.	d. w.	REMARKABLE DAYS.	Sun Rises.		Sun Sets.		Moon Rises.	
			H.	M.	H.	M.	D.	M.
1	mo	Moon's lat. 5 degs. S	5	26	58	4		15
2	tue	Conj. moon with Venus		3	57		sets	
3	we	Vega South, 9 31		4	56	7		27
4	thu	Moon in Apogee,		5	55	7		57
5	fri	Moon on the Equator,		6	54	8		26
6	sat	Day 13h 46m long,		7	53	8		56
7	E	Conj. moon with Saturn		8	52	9		26
8	mo	Moon six days old,		9	51	9		56
9	tue	Battle Cedar Run, '62		10	50	10		30
10	we	Conj. moon Jupiter,		11	49	11		10
11	thu	Lyon's defeat, '61,		12	48	11		56
12	fri	Luna runs low,		13	47		morn	
13	sat	Day's decrease 1h 4m,		14	46	0		48
14	E	12th Sund. after Trinity		15	45	1		50
15	mo	Napoleon born '69,		16	44	2		57
16	tue	Moon's lat. 5° 9' north		17	43	4		8
17	we	Moon fifteen days old		18	42		rises	
18	thu	Moon in Apogee,		19	41	7		15
19	fri	Moon on the Equator,		20	40	7		52
20	sat	Saturn sets 8h. 45m		21	39	8		29
21	E	13th Sunday aft. Trinity		22	38	9		8
22	mo	Bat. Catlett's Station, 62		23	37	9		48
23	tue	Day's decrease 1h. 24m.		24	36	10		33
24	we	Jupiter sets 9h 57m		25	35	11		25
25	thu	Luna runs high		27	33		morn	
26	fri	Day 13h 4m long		28	32	0		18
27	sat	Moon twenty-five d old		29	31	1		13
28	E	Battle near Manassas on		30	30	2		11
29	mo	the 28th and 29th 1862.		31	29	3		10
30	tue	Second bat. Manassas '62		32	28	4		9
31	we	Moon in Apogee,		33	27	5		2

☞A *grave* FACT.—Shuffle the cards as you will, *spades* are sure to win.

Moon's Phases.

	d.	h.	m.	
New Moon	1	1	5	morn.
First Quarter	8	7	6	morn.
Full Moon	5	4	15	after.
Last Quarter	22	6	15	after.
New Moon	30	5	45	after.

d. m.	d. w.	REMARKABLE DAYS.	Sun Rises.		Sun Sets.		Moon Sets.	
			H.	M.	H.	M.	H.	M.
1	thu	Conj. Moon with Venus	5	34	6	26	sets	
2	fri	Altair south 8 55	..	35	..	25	7	4
3	sat	Day 12 48 long	..	36	..	24	7	35
4	E	Conj. Moon with Saturn	..	38	..	22	8	3
5	mo	First Congress met 1774	..	39	..	21	8	36
6	tue	Lafayette born 1757	..	40	..	20	9	13
7	we	Moon six days old	..	41	..	19	9	58
8	thu	Luna runs low	..	42	..	18	10	51
9	fri	Battle Eutaw 1781	..	44	..	16	11	49
10	sat	Battle Lake Erie '13	..	45	..	15	morn
11	E	Battle Brandywine 1777	..	46	..	14	0	53
12	mo	Fomal south 11 31	..	47	..	13	2	0
13	tue	Moon's lat. 5 5 north	..	48	..	12	3	12
14	we	Moon in Perigee	..	49	..	11	4	24
15	thu	Cap. Harper's Ferry '62	..	50	..	10	rises	
16	fri	Moon fifteen days old	..	51	..	9	6	35
17	sat	Battle Sharpsburg '62	..	53	..	7	7	14
18	E	17th Sunday aft. Trinity	..	54	..	6	7	55
19	mo	Altair south 7 56	..	55	..	5	8	42
20	tue	Venus sets 6 44	..	56	..	4	9	30
21	we	Luna runs high	..	58	..	2	10	21
22	thu	Moon 21 days old	..	59	..	1	11	18
23	fri	Autumnal Equinox... }	6	0	..	0	morn
24	sat	Equal day and night.. }	..	1	5	59	0	11
25	E	18th Sunday aft. Trinity	..	3	..	57	1	7
26	mo	Moon's lat. 5 7 south	..	4	..	56	2	6
27	tue	Day's decrease 2 46	..	5	..	55	3	5
28	we	Moon in Apogee	..	7	..	53	3	59
29	thu	St. Michael	..	8	..	52	4	52
30	fri	Altair south 7 17	..	9	..	51	5	47

☞ Men wounded by the explosion of bombshells are wounded *mortarly.*

Moon's Phases.

	d.	h.	m.
First Quarter.........	8	5	43 morn.
Full Moon.............	5	1	15 morn.
Last Quarter	22	9	34 morn.
New Moon.............30	30	10	11 morn

d. m.	d. w.	REMARKABLE DAYS.	Sun Rises	Sun Sets.	Moon sets.
			H. M.	H. M	H. M.
1	sat	Conj. Moon with Saturn	6 10	5 50	sets
2	E	1st Railroad U. S., '33..	.. 11	.. 49	6 42
3	mo	Arcturus south 8 32......	.. 12	.. 48	7 21
4	tue	Conj. Moon with Jupiter	.. 13	.. 47	8 4
5	we	Moon 4 days old...........	.. 14	.. 46	8 51
6	thu	Luna runs low	.. 16	.. 44	9 47
7	fri	Venus sets 6 40............	.. 17	.. 43	10 47
8	sat	Battle Perryville, '62 ...	.. 18	.. 42	11 55
9	E	20th Sunday aft. Trinity	.. 19	.. 41	morn
10	mo	Moon's lat. 5 7 north.....	.. 21	.. 39	1 2
11	tue	Jupiter sets 7 36..........	.. 22	.. 38	2 14
12	we	Moon in Perigee...........	.. 23	.. 37	3 26
13	thu	Battle Queenstown, '12...	.. 24	.. 36	4 38
14	fri	Wm. Penn born, 1644..	.. 26	.. 34	rises
15	sat	Day's decrease 3 30	.. 27	.. 33	5 58
16	E	21st Sunday aft. Trinity	.. 28	.. 32	6 40
17	mo	Day 11 2 long.............	.. 29	.. 31	7 28
18	tue	Luna runs high	.. 30	.. 30	8 19
19	we	Cornwallis surren 1781..	.. 31	.. 29	9 15
20	thu	America discov. 1492....	.. 32	.. 28	10 11
21	fri	Battle Trafalga, '05......	.. 33	.. 27	11 6
22	sat	Fomal south 8 59........	.. 34	.. 26	morn
23	E	Moon enters Virgo	.. 36	.. 24	0 4
24	mo	Dan. Webster died, '52...	.. 37	.. 23	1 0
25	tue	Moon 24 days old.........	.. 38	.. 22	1 56
26	we	Moon in Apogee...........	.. 39	.. 21	2 51
27	thu	Day 10 40 long............	.. 40	.. 20	3 47
28	fri	Saints Simon and Jude..	.. 41	.. 19	4 40
29	sat	Conj. Moon with Saturn	.. 43	.. 17	5 34
30	E	John Adams born, 1735..	.. 44	.. 16	sets
31	mo	Day 10 30 long............	.. 45	.. 15	6 2

Politeness pays about as well as almost anything else that costs as little. Think of it.

Moon's Phases.

	d.	h.	m.
First Quarter	6	2	58 after.
Full Moon	13	0	16 after.
Last Quarter	21	3	36 morn.
New Moon	29	1	51 morn.

d. m.	d. w.	REMARKABLE DAYS.	Sun Rises.		Sun Sets.		Moon Sets.	
			H.	M.	H.	M.	H.	M.
1	tue	Conj. Moon with Venus	6	46	5	14	6	48
2	we	Luna runs low	..	47	..	13	7	38
3	thu	Moon four days old	..	48	..	12	8	38
4	fri	Day 10 h 22 m long	..	49	..	11	9	44
5	sat	Moon's lat. 5 deg. north	..	50	..	10	10	55
6	E	Battle Tippecanoe, '11	..	51	..	9	morn	
7	mo	Venus sets 6 42	..	52	..	8	0	3
8	tue	Moon in Perigree	..	53	..	7	1	12
9	we	Moon on the equator	..	54	..	6	2	22
10	thu	Moon eleven days old	..	55	..	5	3	33
11	fri	Jupiter sets 5 58	..	56	..	4	4	38
12	sat	Day's decrease 4 30	..	57	..	3	5	41
13	E	Meteoric showers of }	..	58	..	2	rises	
14	mo	'33 and '37 }	..	59	..	1	6	12
15	tue	Luna runs high	7	0	..	0	7	2
16	we	Tea destroyed '73	..	1	4	59	7	59
17	thu	Moon eighteen days old.	..	1	..	59	8	55
18	fri	7*s south 12 3	..	2	..	58	9	56
19	sat	Moon's lat. 5 9 south	..	3	..	57	10	48
20	E	26th Sunday aft Trinity	..	4	..	56	11	42
21	mo	Day 9 50 long	..	5	..	55	morn	
22	tue	Sun enters Mars	..	6	..	54	0	36
23	we	Moon 24 days old	..	7	..	53	1	32
24	thu	Z. Taylor born '84	..	7	..	53	2	28
25	fri	Conj. Moon with Saturn	..	8	..	52	3	24
26	sat	Fomal south 6 42	..	9	..	51	4	17
27	E	Advent	..	9	..	51	5	12
28	mo	Sirius rises 9 23	..	10	..	50	6	8
29	tue	Luna runs low	..	11	..	49	sets	
30	we	St. Andrew	..	11	..	49	6	20

Insult not another for his want of a talent you possess: he may have others, which you want. Praise your friends; and let your friends praise you.

Moon's Phases.

	d.	h.	m.
First Quarter	6	1	48 morn.
Full Moon	13	1	47 morn.
Last Quarter	20	10	57 after.
New Moon	28	4	4 after.

d. m.	d. w.	REMARKABLE DAYS.	Sun Rises.	Sun Sets.	Moon Sets.
			H. M.	H. M.	H. M.
1	thu	Conj. Moon with Venus	7 12	4 48	7 23
2	fri	Days decrease five hours	.. 12	.. 48	8 29
3	sat	Moon's lat. 5 9 north	.. 13	.. 47	9 38
4	E	2d Sunday in Advent	.. 13	.. 47	10 50
5	mo	Moon six days old	.. 14	.. 46	morn
6	tue	Moon in Perigee	.. 14	.. 46	0 1
7	we	7*s south 10 43	.. 15	.. 45	1 11
8	thu	Venus sets 7 7	.. 15	.. 45	2 16
9	fri	Moon ten days old	.. 15	.. 45	3 20
10	sat	Saturn rises 3 7 morn	.. 16	.. 44	4 22
11	E	3d Sunday in Advent	.. 16	.. 44	5 22
12	mo	Luna runs high	.. 16	.. 44	6 23
13	tue	Bat. Fredericksburg, '62	.. 17	.. 43	rises
14	we	Washington died, 1799	.. 17	.. 43	6 37
15	thu	Aldeba south 10 56	.. 17	.. 43	7 35
16	fri	Moon's lat. 5 9 south	.. 17	.. 43	8 28
17	sat	Moon eighteen days old	.. 18	.. 42	9 24
18	E	4th Sunday in Advent	.. 18	.. 42	10 20
19	mo	Capella south 11 18	.. 18	.. 42	11 15
20	tue	7*s south 6 46	.. 18	.. 42	morn
21	we	Winter Solstice }	.. 18	.. 42	0 9
22	thu	Shortest day 9 24 }	.. 18	.. 42	1 3
23	fri	Conj. Moon with Saturn	.. 18	.. 42	1 55
24	sat	Moon 25 days old	.. 18	.. 42	2 49
25	E	Christmas Day	.. 18	.. 42	3 46
26	mo	Mason and Slidell relea.	.. 18	.. 42	4 43
27	tue	St. John Evangelist	.. 17	.. 43	5 39
28	we	Venus sets 7 58	.. 17	.. 43	6 37
29	thu	Aldeba south 9 50	.. 17	.. 43	sets
30	fri	Moon's lat. 5 8 north	.. 17	.. 43	7 11
31	sat	Jupiter rises 9 31 morn	.. 17	.. 43	8 15

It is astonishing how keen even stupid people are in discovering imaginary affronts.

Confederate States Government.

LOCATED AT RICHMOND, VA.

The Executive. *Salary.*

Hon JEFF. DAVIS, of Mississippi, *President*........$25,000
Hon. A. H. STEPHENS, of Ga., *Vice-President*........ 6,000

The Cabinet.

J. P. BENJAMIN, of La., *Secretary of State*............. 6,000
C. G. MEMMINGER, of S. C., *Secretary of Treasury*.. 6,000
JAS A. SEDDON, of Va., *Secretary of War*............. 6,000
S. R. MALLORY, of Fla., *Secretary of the Navy*........ 6,000
THOS. H. WATTS, of Ala., *Attorney General*.......... 6,000
JNO. H. REAGAN, of Texas, *Postmaster General*..... 6,000

Heads of Bureaus.

RUFUS R. RHODES, of Miss., Commissioner of Patents.
G. E. W. NELSON, Superintendent of Public Printing.
Gen. SAM. COOPER, Adjutant and Inspector General.
Col. JNO. S. PRESTON, Chief of Bureau of Conscription.
Brig.-Gen. A. R. LAWTON, Quartermaster General.
L. B. NORTHUP, Commissary General.
S. P. MOORE, Surgeon General.
E. W. JOHNS, Medical Purveyor.

Army.
Generals,

SAMUEL COOPER.   R. E. LEE.   JOS. JOHNSTON.
G. T. BEAUREGARD.   BRAXTON BRAGG.

Lieutenant Generals,

JAMES LONGSTREET.   LEONIDAS POLK.   H. I. HARDEE.
E. KIRBY SMITH.   GEO. H. HOLMES.   R. S. EWELL.
J. C. PEMBERTON.   J. C. BRECKINRIDGE. A. P. HILL.

Navy.
Admiral,

FRANKLIN BUCHANAN.

Captains,

L. ROUSSEAU.   FRENCH FORREST.   V. M. RANDOLPH.
G. M. HOLLINS.   D. N. INGRAHAM.   S. BARRON.
J. TATNALL.   W. F. LYNCH.   J. L. STERRETT.
R. SEMMES.

Captains for the War,

S. S. LEE.   W. C. WHITTLE.

SECOND CONGRESS OF CONFEDERATE STATES.

First Session opens Friday, Feb. 19, 1864.

SENATE--26 Members.

VIRGINIA,	ALABAMA,	TEXAS,
R M T Hunter	Ro Jameson	L T Wigfall
A A Caperton	R W Walker	W S Oldham
N. CAROLINA,	**FLORIDA,**	**ARKANSAS,**
W T Dortch	Jas M Baker	R W Johnson
Vacant	E A Maxwell	C B Mitchell
S. CAROLINA,	**MISSISSIPPI,**	**KENTUCKY,**
R W Barnwell	A G Brown	H C Burnett
James L Orr	*J W C Watson	Vacant
GEORGIA,	**LOUISIANA,**	**MISSOURI,**
H V Johnston	Ed Sparrow	R L Y Peyton
B H Hill	T J Semmes	Vacant

TENNESSEE—L C Haynes, G A Henry.

House of Representatives--107 Members.

Virginia,
R L Montague, Robert H Whitfield, Wm C Wickham, Thomas S Gholson, William C Rives, Thomas S Bocock, John Goode, Jr, D C Dejarnette, David Funsten, F W M Holliday, John B Baldwin, Waller R Staples, Fayette McMullen, Samuel Miller, Robert Johnston, Charles W Russell.

North Carolina,
W H N Smith, R R Bridgers, J T Leach, Thomas C Fuller, Josiah Turner, J A Gilmer. S H Chrtstian, J G Ramsay, B S Gaither, G W Logan.

Georgia,
Julian Hartridge, Wm E Smith, Mark H Blauford, Clifford Anderson, John T Shewmake, John H Echols, Jas M Smith, G N Lester, H P Bell, Warren Atkin.

Alabama,
T J Foster, Wm R Smith, W R W Cobb, M H Cruikshank, F S Lyons, W P Chilton, David Clopton, J L Pugh, L S Dickinson.

Mississippi,
John A Orr, W D H Ader, Israel Welsh, H C Chambers, O R Singleton, E Barksdale, J T Lamkin.

Florida,
J B Daukins, R B Hilton.

Texas.
J A Wilcox, C C Herbert, A M Branch, Frank Sexton, J B Baylor, S H Morgan.

Tennessee,
Jos A Heiskell, W G Swan, A S Colyer, John P Murray, Ed A Keeble, H S Foote, Jas McCollum, Thos Menees, J D C Atkins, John V Wright, David M Currin.

General Officers Killed on both sides during the War.

Confederates,

General A S Johnson, Lieut-General T J Jackson. Brigadier-Generals Robert S Garnett, Barnard E Bee, F S Bartow, F K Zollickoffer, Ben McCulloch, James McIntosh, A H Bradden, T W Ashby, Robert Hatton, R Griffith, C S Winder, Samuel Garland, L O'B Branch, Geo B Anderson, J T Hughes, Henry Little, Maxey Gregg, T R R Cobb, J E Rains, Roger Hanson, E F Paxton, E D Tracy, L Tilghman, Martin E Green, Wm D Pender, R B Garnett, J Barksdale, Paul J Semmes, J J Pettigrew, A E Stein, B H Helm, P Smith.

Federals,

Major General Phillip Kearney, Isaac I Stevens, Jesse L Reno, J K T Mansfield, Israel B Richardson, Hiram G Berry, A W Whipple, John F Reynolds.

Brigadier-Generals Nath'l Lyon, F W Lander, W H L Wallace, Thos Williams, H Bohlen, Geo W Taylor, Isaac P Rodman, P A Hackleman, Jas S Jackson, W K Terrill, Geo D Bayard, C F Jackson, Joshua W Sill, E N Kirk, Edm'd Kirby, Geo Boomer, Stephen H Weed, E J Farnsworth, S K Zook, George C Strong, W H Lytle.

The Confederate Forces.

We roughly estimate the number now in the field and rapidly forming for the field, as follows:

Confederate army, proper	350,000
From conscription up to 45 years	80,000
State levies under late call	50,000
Volunteer exempts	35,000
Total forces	515,000

The white males in the Confederate States, between 18 and 45, liable to conscription, exclusive of Maryland, Missouri, Kentucky and Deleware is 1, 115,000. Between the ages of 18 and 45, now called for,.there are in the remaining Southern States over 900,000 men, exclusive of the Border States. Deducting 300,000 sick and disabled from this number, and we still have 600,000 men in and preparing for the field. The slaves of the South will supply us with food, if every man capable of bearing arms should be called to the field.

An estimate of the number of volunteer troops raised in some of the Confederate States previous to the enforcement of the Conscript act:

Alabama	65,000
Georgia	49,000
Florida	17,000
Mississippi	71,000
Texas	48,000
Virginia	82,000
South Carolina	43,000
Maryland	12,000
Tennessee	39,000
Louisiana	27,000
North Carolina	37,000

Population of the Confederate States.

STATES.	Free.	Slaves.	Total.
Virginia	1,097,373	495,826	1,593,190
North Carolina	679,965	328,377	1,004,342
South Carolina	308,166	407,185	715,371
Georgia	615,336	467,461	1,082,797
Florida	81,885	63,809	145,694
Alabama	520,444	435,473	935,917
Mississippi	407,551	479,607	887,158
Louisiana	354,245	312,186	666,431
Arkansas	331,710	109,065	440,775
Texas	415,999	184,956	600,655
Tennessee	859,528	287,112	1,146,640
Kentucky	920,077	224,490	1,145,567
Missouri	1,185,590	115,619	1,301,209
Total	7,777,869	3,918,166	11,669,646

Table of Interest at Six per Cent.

Principal.	One mo			One Yr.		
	D.	C.	M.	D.	C.	M.
One dollar	0	0	5	0	6	0
Two dollars	0	1	0	0	12	0
Three dollars	0	1	5	0	18	0
Four dollars	0	2	0	0	24	0
Five dollars	0	3	5	0	30	0
Six dollars	0	3	0	0	36	0
Seven dollars	0	3	5	0	42	0
Eight dollars	0	4	0	0	48	0
Nine dollars	0	4	5	0	54	0
Ten dollars	0	5	0	0	60	0
Twenty dollars	0	10	0	1	20	0
Thirty dollars	0	15	0	1	80	0
Forty dollars	0	20	0	2	40	0
Fifty dollars	0	25	0	3	00	0
Sixty dollars	0	30	0	3	60	0
Seventy dollars	0	35	0	4	20	0
Eighty dollars	0	40	0	4	80	0
Ninety dollars	0	45	0	5	40	0
One hundred dollars	0	50	0	6	00	0

The interest of any sum in dollars for six days, is the same sum in mills: viz, of $100, 100 mills or ten cents; of 6,600 mills, $6.60, etc. Money at compound interest will double itself in 11 years, 10 months and 22 days.

It is as obliging in company, especially of superiors, to listen attentively, as to talk entertainingly.

Rates of Postage.

On Letters.'

Single letters, not exceeding a half ounce in weight, to any part of the Confederate States, shall be 10 cents.

An additional single rate for each additional half ounce or less.

Drop letters 2 cents each.

In the foregoing cases the postage to be prepaid by stamps or stamped envelopes.

Advertised letters 2 cents each.

On Newspapers.

One cent shall be charged on each newspaper not exceeding three ounces in weight, and for each additional ounce one-half cent additional.

Periodicals published oftener than semi-monthly shall be charged as newspapers.

Regular subscribers to newspapers shall pay their postage quarterly in advance.

On Periodicals.

Periodicals published oftener than semi-monthly shall be charged as newspapers.

Periodicals published monthly, not exceeding 2½ oz. in weight, 2½ cents per quarter, and for every additional ounce or fraction of an ounce, 2½ cents additional per quarter.

Semi-monthly, double the above rates.

Bi-monthly or quarterly, 2 cents an ounce.

On Transient Printed Matter.

Every other newspaper, pamphlet, periodical and magazine, each circular not sealed, handbill and engraving, not exceeding 3 ounces in weight, 2 cents for any distance; 2 cents additional for each additional ounce or less beyond the first three ounces.

In all cases the postage to be prepaid by stamps or stamped envelopes.

List of Governors of States.

Thomas H Watts, Alabama; H Flanagan, Arkansas; Jos E Brown, Georgia; Thomas O Moore, Louisiana; Charles Clark, Mississippi; Zebulon B Vance, North Carolina; Milledge L Bonham, South Carolina; Isham G Harris, Tennessee; Pendleton Murray, Texas; William Smith, Virginia; John Milton, Florida; T C Reynolds, Missouri; Richard Hawes, Kentucky.

SEEING A SNUFF BOX WALK.—As Pat Hogan set enjoying his connubial bliss upon the banks of a southern creek, he espied a turtle emerging from the stream. "Och hone," he exclaimed solemnly, "that iver I should come to America to see a s███f-box walk!"

The Old and New Testament Dissected.

	Old Testament.	New.	Total.
Books	39	27	66
Chapters	929	260	1189
Verses	23.214	7.959	31.173
Words	592.493	181.253	773.692
Letters	2,728,100	838,380	3.566,480

The Apocrapha has 183 chapters, 6,081 verses, 125,180 words. The middle chapter and the leaf in the Bible is the 117th Psalm; the middle verse is the 8th of the 18th Psalm: the middle line is the second book of Chronicles, 4th chapter. 16th verse. The word *and* occurs in the Old Testament 85,543; the same word occurs in the New Testament 10,684 times. The word *Jehovah* occurs 6,855.

Old Testament.—The middle book of the Old Testament is Proverbs; the middle chapter is the 29th of Job; the middle verse is the 2d book of Chronicles, 20th chapter, 23d verse : the least verse is the 1st book of Chronicles, 1st chapter and 1st verse.

New Testament.—The middle book is Thesalonians 2d; the middle chapter is between the 13th and 14th of the Romans; the middle verse is the 17th of the 17th chapter of the Gospel by Saint John.

The 21st verse of the 7th chapter of Ezra, has all the letters of the Alphabet in it.

The 19th chapter of the 2d book of Kings, and the 37th chapter of Isaiah are alike.

The book of Esther has ten chapters, but neither the word *Lord* or *God* in it.

Population of the Earth.

A professor of the University of Berlin has recently published the result of his researches as to the population of the earth. according to which Europe contains 272 millions. Asia 720 millions, Africa 89 millions, America 200 millions and Polynesia 2 millions, making a grand total of 1,283 millions of inhabitants.

At places where deaths are accurately registered, the the annual mortality is at least one in forty ; the number of deaths must be about 32 millions every year which gives 87,761 per day, 2,653 per hour, and 60 per minute, so that every second witnesses the extinction of one human life. Another calculator states that the number of persons who have lived on the earth since the creation is 36,627,740,275,075,855!

Two citizens courting the daughter of Themistocles, he preferred the worthy man to the rich one, and assigned the reason, "I had rather she should have a man without money, than money without a man."

He who knows the world will not be too bashful. He who knows himself will not be impudent.

Chronology of Important Inventions.

Maps, globes and dials were first invented by Anaximander, in the sixth century before Christ. They were first brought into England by Bartholomew Columbus in 1489.

Comedy and Tragedy were first exhibited at Athens, 562 B C.

Plays were first acted at Rome. 239 B C.

Paper was invented in China. 170 B C.

The Calendar was reformed by Julius Cæsar. 45 B C.

Insurance on ships and merchandise first made in A D 43.

Manufacture of silk brought from India into Europe, 551 A D.

Pens first made of quills. A D 635.

Stone buildings and glass introduced into England. A D 674.

The figures of Arifhmetic brought into Europe by the Saracens. A D 991.

Paper of cotton rags invented towards the close of the tenth century.

Paper made of linen in 1300.

The degree of doctor first conferred in Europe, at Bologna. in 1130; in England in 1209.

Astronomy and Geometry brought into England. 1220.

Linen first made in England. 1253.

Spectacles invented. 1280.

The art of weaving introduced into England. 1330.

Gunpowder invented at the city of Cologne, by Schwat, 1320.

Cannon first used at the siege of Algeziras. 1342.

Muskets in use. 1370.

Pistols in use. 1544.

Printing invented at Mentz, by Guttemberg, 1440.

Printing introduced into England. 1471.

Post Offices established in France, 1464; in England. 1581; in Germany, 1640.

First coach made in England. 1564.

Clocks first made in England, 1568.

DIARY FOR 1864.

Friday, January 1st.

Saturday 2nd,

Sunday 3d.

Monday 4th.

B

Tuesday, 5th.

Wednesday, 6th.

Thursday, 7th.

Friday, 8th.

Saturday, 9th.

Sunday, 10th.

Monday 11th.

Tuesday, 12th.

Wednesday, 13th.

Thursday 14th.

Friday, 15th.

Saturday 16th.

Sunday, 17th.

Monday, 18th.

Tuesday, 19th.

Wednesday, 20th.

Thursday, 21st.

Friday, 22nd.

Saturday, 23rd.

Sunday, 24th.

Monday, 25th.

Tuesday, 26th.

Wednesday, 27th.

Thursday, 28th.

Friday, 29th.

Saturday, 30th.

Sunday, 31st.

Monday, 1st

Aplied to Dr Watson

Tuesday, 2nd.

Mr R Turner — 4 barrels corn

Wm H. Harris 35. barrels

I D Harrar — 4 or 3 per mo
commensing first of march

Wednesday, 3rd.

B G Harris 15 barrels

Thursday, 4th.

Friday, 5th

I Robert Kennedes
15 bushels corn

Saturday, 6th.

Sunday, 7th.

Monday, 8th.

Tuesday, 9th.

Wednesday, 10th.

Thursday, 11th.

Friday, 12th.

Saturday, 13th.

Sunday, 14th.

Monday, 15th.

Tuesday, 16th.

Wednesday, 17th.

Thursday, 18th.

Friday, 19th.

Saturday, 20th.

Sunday, 21st.

Monday, 22nd.

Tuesday, 23rd.

Wednesday, 24th.

Thursday, 25th.

Friday, 26th.

Saturday, 27th.

Sunday, 28th.

Monday, 29th.

Tuesday, 1st.

Wednesday, 2nd.

Thursday, 3rd.

Friday, 4th.

Saturday, 5th.

Sunday, 6th.

Monday, 7th.

Tuesday, 8th.

Wednesday, 9th.

Thursday, 10th.

Friday, 11th.

Saturday, 12th.

Sunday, 13th.

Monday, 14th.

Tuesday, 15th.

Wednesday, 16th.

Thursday, 17th.

Friday, 18th.

Saturday, 19th.

Sunday, 20th.

Monday, 21st.

Tuesday, 22d.

Wednesday, 23d.

Thursday, 24th.

Friday, 25th.

Saturday, 26th.

Sunday, 27th.

Monday, 28th.

Tuesday, 29th.

Thursday, 31st.

.   .

.

April, 1861.

Friday, 1st.

Saturday, 2nd.

Sunday, 3rd.

Monday, 4th.

Tuesday, 5th.

Wednesday, 6th.

Thursday, 7th.

Friday, 8th.

Saturday, 9th.

Sunday, 10th.

Monday, 11th.

Tuesday, 12th.

Wednesday, 13th.

Thursday, 14th.

Friday, 15th.

April. 1864.

Saturday, 16th.

Sunday, 17th.

Monday, 18th.

Tuesday, 19th.

Wednesday, 20th.

Thursday, 21st.

Friday, 22nd.

Saturday, 23rd.

Sunday, 24th.

Monday, 25th.

Tuesday, 26th.

Wednesday, 27th.

Thursday, 28*th.*

Friday, 29*th.*

Saturday, 30*th.*

Sunday, 1st.

Monday, 2nd.

Tuesday, 3rd.

Wednesday, 4th.

Thursday, 5th.

Friday, 6th.

Saturday, 7th.

Sunday, 8th.

Monday, 9th.

Tuesday, 10th.

Wednesday, 11th.

Thursday, 12th.

Friday, 13*th.*

Saturday, 14*th.*

Sunday, 15*th.*

Monday, 16*th.*

Tuesday, 17*th.*

Wednesday, 18*th.*

C·

Thursday, 19th.

Friday, 20th.

Saturday, 21st.

Sunday, 22d.

Monday, 23d.

Tuesday, 24th.

Wednesday, 25th.

Thursday, 26th.

Friday, 27th.

Saturday, 28th.

Sunday, 29th.

Monday, 30th.

Tuesday, 31st.

June, 1864.

Wednesday, 1st.

Thursday, 2d.

Friday, 3d.

Saturday, 4th.

'

Sunday, 5th.

`

Monday, 6th.

Tuesday, 7th.

Wednesday, 8th.

•

Thursday, 9th.

Friday, 10th.

Saturday, 11th.

Sunday, 12th.

Monday, 13th.

Tuesday, 14th.

Wednesday, 15th.

Thursday, 16th.

Friday, 17th.

Saturday, 18th.

Sunday, 19th.

Monday, 20th.

Tuesday, 21st.

Wednesday, 22d.

Thursday, 23d.

Friday, 24th.

Saturday, 25th.

Sunday, 26th.

Monday, 27th.

Tuesday, 28th.

Wednesday, 29th.

Thursday, 30th.

Friday. 1st

Saturday, 2d.

Sunday, 3d.

Monday, 4th.

Tuesday, 5th.

Wednesday, 6th.

Thursday, 7th.

Friday, 8th.

Saturday, 9th.

Sunday, 10th.

Monday, 11th.

Tuesday, 12th.

Wednesday, 13th.

Thursday, 14th.

Friday, 15th.

Saturday, 16th.

Sunday, 17th.

Monday, 18th.

Tuesday 19th.

Wednesday, 20th.

Thursday. 21st.

Friday, 22d.

.

Saturday, 23d.

Sunday, 24th.

July. 1864.

Monday, 25th.

Tuesday, 26th.

Wednesday, 27th.

Thursday, 28th.

Friday, 29th.

Saturday, 30th.

Sunday, 31st.

August, 1864.

Monday, 1st.

Tuesday, 2d.

Wednesday, 3d.

Thursday, 4th.

Friday, 5th.

Saturday, 6th.

Sunday, 7th.

Monday, 8th.

Tuesday, 9th.

Wednesday, 10th.

Thursday, 11th.

Friday. 12th.

Saturday, 13th.

Sunday, 14th.

Monday, 15th.

Tuesday, 16th.

Wednesday, 17th.

Thursday, 18th.

Friday, 19th.

Saturday, 20th.

Sunday, 21st.

Monday 22d.

Tuesday, 23d.

Wednesday, 24th.

Thursday, 25th.

Friday, 26th.

Saturday, 27th.

Sunday, 28th.

Monday, 29th.

Tuesday, 30th.

Wednesday, 31st.

Thursday. 1st.

Friday, 2d.

Saturday, 3rd.

Sunday, 4th.

Monday, 5th.

Tuesday, 6th.

September. 1864.

Wednesday 7th.

Thursday, 8th.

Friday, 9th.

Saturday 10th.

Sunday, 11th.

Monday 12th.

Tuesday, 13th.

.

Wednesday, 14th.

Thursday, 15th.

Friday, 16th. .

Saturday, 17th.

Sunday, 18th.

Monday 19th.

Tuesday, 20th.

Wednesday, 21st.

Thursday, 22d.

Friday, 23rd.

Saturday 24th.

Sunday, 25th.

Monday, 26th.

Tuesday, 27th.

Wednesday, 28th.

Thursday, 29th.

Friday, 30th.

D.

Sunday, 2d.

Monday, 3d.

Tuesday, 4th.

.

Wednesday, 5th.

Thursday, 6th.

Friday, 7th.

Saturday, 8th.

.

Sunday, 9th.

Monday, 10th.

Tuesday, 11th.

Wednesday, 12th.

Thursday, 13*th.*

Friday, 14*th.*

Saturday, 15*th.*

Sunday, 16*th.*

Monday, 17*th.*

Tuesday, 18*th.*

Wednesday, 19th.

Thursday, 20th.

Friday, 21st.

Saturday, 22d.

Sunday, 23d.

Monday, 24th.

Tuesday, 25th.

Wednesday, 26th.

Thursday, 27th.

Friday, 28th.

Saturday, 29th.

Sunday, 30th.

Monday, 31st.

November, 1864.

Tuesday, 1st.

Wednesday, 2d.

Thursday, 3d

Friday, 4th.

Saturday, 5th.

Sunday, 6th.

Monday, 7th.

Tuesday, 8th.

Wednesday, 9th.

Thursday, 10th.

Friday, 11th.

Saturday, 12th.

Sunday, 13th.

Monday, 14th.

Tuesday, 15th.

Wednesday, 16th.

Thursday, 17th.

Friday, 18th.

Saturday 19th.

Sunday, 20th.

Monday, 21st.

Tuesday, 22d.

Wednesday, 23rd.

Thursday, 24th.

Friday, 25th.

Saturday, 26th.

Sunday, 27th.

Monday, 28th

Tuesday, 29th.

Wednesday, 30th.

Thursday, 1st.

Friday, 2d.

Saturday, 3rd.

Sunday, 4th.

Monday, 5th.

Tuesday, 6th.

Wednesday, 7th.

Thursday, 8th.

Friday, 9th.

Saturday, 10th.

Sunday, 11th.

Monday, 12th.

Tuesday, 13th.

l

Wednesday, 14th.

Thursday, 15th.

Friday, 16th.

Saturday, 17th.

Sunday, 18th.

Monday, 19th.

Tuesday, 20th.

Wednesday, 21st.

Thursday, 22d.

Friday, 23d.

Saturday, 24th.